501 Would You Rather Questions

Funny, gross, challenging, awkward, painful and random questions for all ages

Stephen Pepper

ISBN: 1519502672
ISBN-13: 978-1519502674

HOW TO PLAY WOULD YOU RATHER

Would You Rather is an excellent game for all occasions and for all ages. It can be funny, informative, challenging, embarrassing and so much more.

Best of all, it's simple to play – all you need to do is pick a question and ask the players which of the two options they'd rather choose.

If you want, you can then ask one or more of the players why they chose the option that they did. This is particularly useful when playing Would You Rather with children or teens as it can help you learn more about them, their likes and dislikes and also how their mind works.

HOW TO PLAY WITH A GROUP

If you have a large group of players, it might not be feasible to ask each person individually for their answer.

Instead, here are some different ways in which you can get players in the group to signify their answers:

- Stand to the left for one option and to the right for the other
- Hold up one hand for the first option or both hands for the second option
- Stand on one leg for one option and touch their nose for the other
- Sit down for one option and lay on the floor for the other

- Stick their tongue out for one option and wave their hands over their head for the other
- Use two different colored post-it notes, sticking one color on their forehead for one option and the other color on their chin for the second choice

You can therefore make the game as wild and wacky as your imagination allows!

WOULD YOU RATHER TIPS

- Make sure players know that there are no right or wrong answers – it's all about their preferences
- If you have any indecisive players, consider putting a time limit on how long they have to choose their answer
- Be sensitive with the questions you pick depending on who's playing. For example, if somebody recently suffered a bereavement, it might be best not to choose a question about death.
- If working with young people, consider asking the same question at both the start and end of a session to see if their perception was changed by the discussion. For example, asking "Would you rather marry someone rich who cheats on you or someone with no money who is faithful?" at the end of a session about healthy relationships might elicit a different response compared to how they would have answered before the discussion.

Would You Rather...

1

...have Christmas be cold and snowy or hot and sunny?

2

...learn sign language or a foreign language?

3

...swap your feet for wheels or your hands for Swiss Army Knives?

4

...be in front of 100 people to dance or give a speech?

5

...climb Mt Everest or walk the entire length of the Great Wall of China?

6

...take one vacation that lasts four weeks or four vacations that each last one week?

7

...eat no candy at Halloween or no turkey at Thanksgiving?

8

...make a small difference in the lives of ten people or a massive difference in the life of one person?

9

...clean the floor with a toothbrush or mow the yard with a pair of scissors?

10

...be able to cut bushes so that they look like animals or carve ice sculptures?

11

...shiver when you're hot or sweat when you're cold?

12

...be killed but have everyone think you're a hero or stay alive but have everyone think you're a coward?

13

...have a real or artificial Christmas tree?

14

...eat ramen noodles topped with jam or celery dipped in chocolate pudding?

15

...be on an empty beach when it's cloudy or on a busy beach when it's sunny?

16

...buy Christmas gifts online or in a store?

17

...listen to the same song all day every day for seven days or not listen to any music for a year?

18

...swim with dolphins or ride an elephant?

19

...eat beef jerky covered in blueberry yogurt or ravioli covered with strawberry milkshake?

20

...be able to fly or be invisible?

21

...have a time machine or be able to walk on water?

22

...have no homework for the rest of your life or no exams?

23

...have to dig a 10 foot hole or build a 20 foot wall?

24

...be bitten by a shark or attacked by a swarm of bees?

25

...watch movies or play video games for 48 hours?

26

...have purple or green hair?

27

...have seven fingers on each hand or seven toes on each foot?

28

...go grocery shopping or make dinner?

29

...have an apple tree or orange tree growing in your yard?

30

...have a red or blue car?

31

...work on a cruise ship or an airplane?

32

...be in a cave full of bats or a room full of cockroaches?

33

...build a fort or climb a tree?

34

...have a guy or a girl as your best friend?

35

...be given a wedgie or have sand thrown in your eyes?

36

...receive five Valentine's Day cards but not know who they're from or receive one Valentine's Day card and know who sent it?

37

...go to a water park or theme park?

38

...be trapped for an hour in a room full of mosquitoes or rats?

39

...save money or spend it?

40

...get famous quickly as a reality TV star or earn an Oscar when you're 75?

41

...have a stone in your shoe or an eyelash in your eye?

42

...have three arms or three legs?

43

...not shower for a month or not change your clothes for a month?

44

...ride in a limousine or a Ferrari?

45

...drink orange juice or apple juice?

46

...watch TV sitting on a sofa or lying in bed?

47

...eat liver or kidney?

48

...make snow angels or go sledding?

49

...spend 15 minutes standing on one leg or lifting one arm above your head?

50

...be able to fly like a reindeer or be able to squeeze down a chimney?

51

...have your nose grow when you tell a lie or have everything you touch turn to ice?

52

...eat M&Ms or Skittles?

53

...eat a cockroach or drink a squished slug?

54

...be woken up by a dog that barks loudly or licks your face?

55

...go bobbing for apples in a toilet or drink some bath water after someone has just washed in it?

56

...have dirty hands or sticky hands?

57

...be able to lay eggs or shed your skin?

58

...wash 20 cars or pick up trash for 5 hours?

59

...run in a hamster wheel or a hamster ball?

60

...go to Paris for Valentine's Day or the North Pole for Christmas?

61

...be a fish or a bird?

62

...forget how to speak or how to walk?

63

...have a vending machine that dispensed any food you wanted whenever you wanted it or a machine that could teleport you to anywhere you wanted to go?

64

...be a teacher or a principal?

65

...be a magician or a clown?

66

...have to walk a mile-long balance beam or have to climb up and over a 100 foot high cargo net?

67

...have every day be Halloween or Thanksgiving?

68

...listen to someone eating with their mouth open or cracking their knuckles?

69

...go on vacation at a 5 star hotel for two nights or a 3 star hotel for seven nights?

70

...milk a cow or shear a sheep?

71

...have someone wake you up in the morning or be woken by an alarm clock?

72

...slide down the pole at a fire station or take a ride on a fire engine while the sirens are going?

73

...eat cottage cheese with olives in it or tomato soup with cheese puffs in it?

74

...be able to build a house or a website?

75

...sit by the window or in an aisle seat on an airplane?

76

...have someone tickle your feet or under your arms?

77

...have to kill an animal any time you want to eat meat or never eat meat again?

78

...live in a world without mirrors or shelves?

79

...have a tennis court or basketball court in your backyard?

80

...meet Buzz Lightyear or Shrek?

81

...have to dress like a Pilgrim or a Native American for a week?

82

...live on a boat or in an RV?

83

...paint a picture or create a sculpture?

84

...be a wedding photographer or a wedding planner?

85

...have one piece of homework that takes five hours to complete or five pieces of homework that each take one hour to complete?

86

...play on a trampoline or a bounce house?

87

...eat five onions or five lemons?

88

...go to bed every night at 8pm or 2am?

89

...be locked out of your house or your car?

90

...only eat fruit or vegetables for one year?

91

...work in an office with lots of people or at home by yourself?

92

...have one 12 hour flight or two 8 hour flights to get to your vacation destination?

93

...visit Japan or Brazil?

94

...live without running water or electricity?

95

...be an elephant or a rhinoceros?

96

...have a fly stuck in your ear or 100 ants in your underwear?

97

...be trapped in a giant cobweb or get stuck in quicksand?

98

...walk a tightrope or be a lion tamer?

99

...go on a zip-line over the Grand Canyon or sit on the roof's edge of the world's tallest building?

100

...listen to a baby scream for two hours or change twenty dirty diapers?

101

...play on a swing or a seesaw?

102

...sleep for three days while everyone else is awake or be awake for three days while everyone else is asleep?

103

...travel across the US by train or by car?

104

...live underwater or underground?

105

...take a bath in honey or ketchup?

106

...wake up and meet the tooth fairy but don't get any money for your tooth or stay asleep and have it leave you $100 for your tooth?

107

...wear handcuffs for 48 hours attached to your wrists or your ankles?

108

...get a tattoo or a piercing?

109

...have a tail or four legs?

110

...go to jail for a crime you didn't commit or have your best friend go to jail for a crime that you committed?

111

...be in a band that no one likes or be part of a sports team that always loses?

112

...suffer from hay fever or be allergic to cats and dogs?

113

...spend Christmas Day with Frosty The Snowman or The Grinch?

114

...walk all the way up the stairs in the Empire State Building or abseil down the outside of it?

115

...only be able to shout or whisper?

116

...be able to change your skin like a chameleon or run as fast as a cheetah?

117

...peel 500 potatoes or wash 2,000 plates by hand?

118

...get your fingers trapped in a door or step on a nail?

119

...go back in time 100 years or go forward in time 100 years?

120

...be a ninja or a spy?

121

...meet the President of the USA or your favorite singer?

122

...be a teacher or a doctor?

123

...listen to bells chiming non-stop for 24 hours or the song you hate the most on repeat for three hours?

124

...be buried or cremated?

125

...work fifteen hours per day three days a week or nine hours per day five days a week?

126

...live without music or without TV and movies for the rest of your life?

127

...sweat loads but not smell or smell but not sweat?

128

...go waterskiing or jet skiing?

129

...have to eat ten spiders or two scorpions?

130

...receive one big gift at Christmas or ten small gifts?

131

...be a plumber or electrician?

132

...play beach volleyball or beach soccer?

133

...watch TV or read a book?

134

...get a splinter or a papercut?

135

...fall off a galloping horse or off your bike when riding downhill?

136

...stroke a tarantula or a snake?

137

...not be able to stop burping or farting?

138

...be able to pilot a plane or fly a helicopter?

139

...live on a boat and never step foot on land again or live in a large house but never step foot outside again?

140

...forget how to count or how to spell?

141

...have an egg cracked on your head or a gallon of milk poured over you?

142

...have to permanently wear swimming goggles or a mouthguard?

143

...have a light bulb appear over your head whenever you have an idea or have speech bubbles appear whenever you say something?

144

...be sprayed with a fire hose or shot with a paintball gun?

145

...have to wear wet clothes or wet shoes?

146

...have to use candles to see in the dark or use a fireplace to keep warm when it's cold?

147

...be able to move objects with your mind or make them disappear?

148

...know how you'll die or when you'll die?

149

...eat a teaspoon of black pepper or a teaspoon of salt?

150

...walk barefoot in snow or on hot sand?

151

...eat a curry in India or pasta in Italy?

152

...win ten silver medals or one gold medal at the Olympic Games?

153

...have someone sneeze all over your hair or have someone else's pimple burst over your face?

154

...live without forks or spoons?

155

...iron 30 shirts or make dinner for your family every day for a month?

156

...have a maid who cleans your house or a chef who makes all your meals?

157

...experience life in slow motion or fast forward?

158

...be a ballet dancer or an opera singer?

159

...have to wear a school uniform or have your parents pick out what you have to wear each day?

160

...know who's naughty or nice and have to give coal if you're Santa or not know and give everyone gifts even if they don't deserve it?

161

...work 40 hours a week working for someone else or 80 hours a week owning your own business?

162

...climb up a ladder that has 250 steps or down a ladder that has 1,000 steps?

163

...have your head be the size of a yoga ball or a tennis ball?

164

...jump in puddles during a storm or stay inside in the dry?

165

...complete a crossword or a jigsaw puzzle?

166

...have someone catch you singing or dancing?

167

...meet Snow White or Cinderella?

168

...sleep with a pillow but no blanket or with a blanket but no pillow?

169

...have a water balloon fight or go on a Slip 'N Slide?

170

...have your best friend die or have them become a zombie?

171

...be too hot or too cold?

172

...go camping in a forest or on a mountain?

173

...be scared of dust or the number 8?

174

...have it snow every day during winter or have no snow at all?

175

...have skin like a pineapple or a coconut?

176

...be one of the dwarfs in Snow White or one of Robin Hood's Merry Men?

177

...be a scarecrow with no brains or a tinman with no heart?

178

...be able to walk through walls or breathe underwater?

179

...brush your teeth with a hairbrush or brush your hair with a toothbrush?

180

...be able to see through walls or hear things from miles away?

181

...have a shower under a waterfall or a bath in a hot spring?

182

...be Santa and have to eat all the cookies and milk or be the reindeers and have to eat all the vegetables?

183

...be stuck in an elevator or on a ski lift?

184

...iron clothes or vacuum the house?

185

...try to catch a fish with a spear or a deer with a boomerang?

186

...roll around in horse poop which doesn't smell or wear deodorant which makes you smell like horse poop?

187

...make 100 beds or clean 10 toilets?

188

...get hit on the arm by a baseball or in the stomach by a football?

189

...throw water balloons at your parents or your teachers?

190

...climb a tree or roll down a sand dune?

191

...read a book or listen to an audio book?

192

...drive a car or ride a motorcycle?

193

...paint the walls of two rooms or clean all the windows of a house?

194

...try to swim in macaroni and cheese or potato salad?

195

...know everything or know nothing?

196

...be able to communicate with trees or birds?

197

...have it be 32°F or 110°F every day?

198

...always say everything that you think or only be able to answer questions by saying "Yes"?

199

...hit your thumb with a hammer or get sunburnt?

200

...live opposite a cemetery or in an abandoned amusement park?

201

...live in a massive house by yourself or a tiny house with ten friends?

202

...work from 5am to 2pm or from 1pm to 10pm?

203

...be able to teleport or see into the future?

204

...high-five a cactus or kick a rock while barefoot?

205

...play soccer or basketball?

206

...eat two big meals a day or four smaller meals?

207

...live next to an airport or a train line?

208

...be part of a float at the Macy's Thanksgiving Day parade and appear on TV or stay home and watch football on TV?

209

...pose in the window of a clothing store or dance with a mannequin?

210

...steal a baby's toy or an old person's walking stick?

211

...be a trapeze artist or a human cannonball?

212

...be rich or powerful?

213

...drive a dune buggy or go go-karting?

214

...relax on a bean bag or in a hammock?

215

...have bad breath or stinky feet?

216

...play with a puppy or kitten?

217

...write a story where the characters come alive in real life or paint a picture that you can jump in to?

218

...eat turkey or ham at Thanksgiving?

219

...fall asleep listening to waves crashing on the beach or animals in the jungle?

220

...have to get a vaccination every day for a year or have 365 vaccinations in one day?

221

...chew gum or eat mints?

222

...never be able to say thank you or please?

223

...don't eat anything for two days or eat too much and throw up?

224

...drive a tank or fly a fighter jet?

225

...win $5 million tomorrow or $100 million in 20 years' time?

226

...win a dream two week vacation or a $10,000 shopping spree in your favorite store?

227

...play football or baseball?

228

...burp or hiccup once every minute?

229

...have your dream house or your dream car?

230

...be the world's best diver or fastest swimmer?

231

...see a bear or a rattlesnake while camping?

232

...have a pet starfish called Ermentrude or a pet seahorse called Donut?

233

...drive a beautiful brand new car which keeps breaking down or drive an ugly 25 year old car which never breaks down?

234

...walk 50 miles or jog 10 miles?

235

...be stuck on a broken rollercoaster or walk into a haunted house by yourself?

236

...have no one attend your wedding or your funeral?

237

...watch a firework display or a meteor shower?

238

...be able to read someone's mind or make them forget things?

239

...sleep on a bed made of Lego or sit on a sofa made of pebbles?

240

...be able to ride a unicycle or walk on stilts?

241

...be a movie star or a rock star?

242

...be a car mechanic or build houses for a living?

243

...drink warm water or hot chocolate that's gone cold?

244

...not be invited to a party which all your friends are going to or go to a party where you don't know anyone?

245

...not have to eat or not have to sleep?

246

...have all your hair fall out overnight or wake up covered in hair all over your body?

247

...drink Dr Pepper or Sprite?

248

...be able to remember everything you see or everything you hear?

249

...be the world's fastest runner or swimmer?

250

...eat fried chicken or a burger?

251

...watch a sunrise or a sunset?

252

...have someone shout at you or ignore you?

253

...earn money clearing snow from a neighbor's driveway or have a snowball fight with friends?

254

...be an animal confined in an enclosure at a zoo where it's safe or be free in the wild but have predators hunting you?

255

...come across a vampire or a werewolf?

256

...be able to play the piano or guitar?

257

...get to stay in bed for an extra hour each morning or finish school or work an hour earlier each afternoon?

258

...get stung by a wasp or pricked by a cactus?

259

...live in a castle or a huge tree house?

260

...drink orange juice and milk mixed together in a glass or bacon fat?

261

...make a sand castle or be buried in the sand?

262

...own a magic wand or a flying broomstick?

263

...be stuck for two days in an airport or for four days in a hotel that has no running water?

264

...be abducted by aliens or trapped in a submarine at the bottom of the ocean?

265

...jump in the biggest pile of leaves you've ever seen or have a snowball fight?

266

...have been Christopher Columbus or George Washington?

267

...sneeze every five minutes or cry every five minutes?

268

...have a yellow tongue or orange eyes?

269

...go to school from 8am to 3pm or 11am to 6pm?

270

...have every day be your birthday or Christmas Day?

271

...be 3 feet or 9 feet tall?

272

...learn Spanish or French?

273

...live in a gingerbread house or have magic beans?

274

...go to jail for ten years or be on the run for the rest of your life?

275

...know what gifts you're getting at Christmas or have it be a surprise?

276

...go on a safari in Africa or kayaking in Antarctica?

277

...eat chocolate ice cream or vanilla ice cream?

278

...earn lots of money doing a job you hate or not earn much doing a job you love?

279

...never eat pizza or burgers again?

280

...watch a movie that makes you laugh or makes you cry?

281

...have the nickname Cupcake or Twinkie?

282

...have oversized feet or oversized hands?

283

...break an arm or leg?

284

...be a pirate or a cowboy?

285

...faint at your wedding or your high school graduation?

286

...travel by hovercraft or sailboat?

287

...play Frisbee or fly a kite?

288

...clean the outside or inside of a car?

289

...fall flat on your face in front of someone you have a huge crush on or live on national television?

290

...be in a haunted house or on a ghost ship?

291

...wear shoes or flip-flops?

292

...travel somewhere using a jetpack or by being able to run at 200 mph?

293

...say yes to everything for a month or no to everything for a month?

294

...have hot feet or hot hands?

295

...be as tall as a house or as small as an ant?

296

...look for a needle in a haystack or have to count the number of words in a long novel?

297

...eat shrimp covered in oatmeal or mashed banana with onions mixed in?

298

...be able to jump as high as a skyscraper or climb up the outside of a skyscraper like Spiderman?

299

...sleep on the floor or sitting upright in a chair?

300

...break a mirror or have a black cat cross your path?

301

...win the long jump or the high jump at the Olympic Games?

302

...have someone drop ice down the back of your T-shirt or tickle your feet?

303

...see mountain gorillas in the wild in Rwanda or go scuba diving in the Great Barrier Reef in Australia?

304

...blow up 100 balloons by mouth or lick 500 envelopes to seal them?

305

...watch a lightning storm or a firework display?

306

...be able to run 100 mph or be able to drop from any height and land on your feet without getting hurt?

307

...meet a zombie or Frankenstein's monster?

308

...be famous and have no friends or not famous with many friends?

309

...faint whenever you see blood or look at a mirror and see someone different looking back at you?

310

...be the subject of a famous painting or a famous song?

311

...have no children or have ten children?

312

...live in a house with four walls but no roof or one which has no walls but a canopy overhead?

313

...only drink water or grapefruit juice for the rest of your life?

314

...always feel tired or always feel hungry?

315

...play ping pong with a tennis ball or baseball with a soccer ball?

316

...skim rocks on a lake or play in sand at the beach?

317

...live in a world with no toilet paper or no soap?

318

...step into a muddy puddle or have a car drive through it and splash you?

319

...hit the game-winning home run in the World Series or score the winning touchdown in the Super Bowl?

320

...jump in a puddle or a pile of leaves?

321

...fly on a broomstick or a magic carpet?

322

...be homeless or in prison?

323

...live in a world with no trees or no flowers?

324

...be a nurse or a veterinarian?

325

...have your favorite band break up or your favorite restaurant close down?

326

...invent something amazing but have someone else take the credit for it or have someone else invent it but you take credit for inventing it?

327

...cheat on a test and get an A or not cheat and get an F?

328

...go to school for 5 days a week for 13 years or for 2.5 days a week for 26 years?

329

...be able to jump along like a kangaroo or swing like a monkey?

330

...fight a tiger or a bear?

331

...fart in an elevator and have everyone know it was you or pee in a swimming pool which has dye in it so everyone knows it was you?

332

...eat a burrito or taco?

333

...bite someone else's fingernails or pick their nose?

334

...sleep on a bed with no pillow or on the floor with a pillow?

335

...have every day be warm and cloudy or cold and sunny?

336

...sleep in or wake up early on Christmas Day?

337

...not brush your teeth for two weeks or not shower for a month?

338

...become President of the USA or be the first person to step foot on Mars?

339

...live on the 12th floor of a building that has no elevator or in a house that has no windows?

340

...spend a year all by yourself or not having any time alone?

341

...be famous for doing something embarrassing or not be famous at all?

342

...be God and have no one believe in you or not be God but have everyone believe you are?

343

...eat dry dog food or wet cat food?

344

...keep a secret from your best friend or have your best friend keep a secret from you?

345

...meet Santa Claus or the Easter Bunny?

346

...carry two bricks for two miles or four bricks for one mile?

347

...be blind or deaf?

348

...sleep outside for the night on the beach or on the roof of a skyscraper?

349

...be stranded on a desert island by yourself with lots of different things to eat or with your best friend but only having rice to eat?

350

...be kept awake at night by a dog barking or be woken up early by a cock crowing?

351

...watch a meteor shower or solar eclipse?

352

...be able to shine light from the tips of your fingers or spray water from your toes?

353

...only eat ice cream or pizza for the rest of your life?

354

...have carpet or hardwood floors in your bedroom?

355

...have a two week vacation on a remote island or go on a cruise?

356

...be able to put Humpty Dumpty together again or stop Jack and Jill from falling down the hill?

357

...be Spiderman or Batman?

358

...take a shower or bath?

359

...own a coffee shop or a restaurant?

360

...walk into a door while people are watching or drop your dinner in your lap at a restaurant?

361

...marry someone rich who cheats on you or someone with no money who is faithful?

362

...earn millions creating a cure for a disease that only saves 1,000 people or earn no money creating a cure for a disease that saves five million people?

363

...be able to make paper airplanes that can fly one mile or be able to blow a bubble the size of a person?

364

...have grass be purple or the sky be green?

365

...be able to kick or throw a ball 200 yards?

366

...get married to someone you don't love or have to do a job you hate for the rest of your life?

367

...wear jeans back to front for a month or shoes on the opposite feet for a week?

368

...be the singer performing the halftime show at the Super Bowl or be a quarterback playing in it?

369

...go in a hot air balloon or a blimp?

370

...have no fingers or no toes?

371

...have to eat Thanksgiving dinner with baseball mitts on each hand or open your Christmas gifts with boxing gloves on?

372

...have a baby throw up on you or pee on you?

373

...be able to touch your forehead with your tongue or be able to touch your left elbow with your left hand?

374

...grow vegetables or colorful flowers in your yard?

375

...stay in a sleazy motel on the oceanfront or a luxury hotel with nothing to do nearby?

376

...lick the sidewalk in Times Square or the toilet seat at home?

377

...have one teacher for all your classes who's average or different teachers for each subject, half of whom are great and the other half being awful?

378

...be 5 or 35 years old?

379

...fly in a helicopter or go underwater in a submarine?

380

...only be allowed to eat your meals with chopsticks or with your fingers?

381

...make a Valentine's Day card by hand or buy one from the store?

382

...have a dinosaur or a dolphin as a pet?

383

...ask someone on a date and have them say no or never ask them and so never know?

384

...be scared of heights or spiders?

385

...live by the beach or in the mountains?

386

...change four tires on a car by yourself or walk ten miles to get gas after your car breaks down due to an empty tank?

387

...spend one hour on Mars or a week on the moon?

388

...get married on the beach or in a church?

389

...be a bird that can't fly or a fish that can't swim?

390

...be a police officer or firefighter?

391

...smell freshly cut grass or freshly baked bread?

392

...have a baby boy or a baby girl?

393

...use tortilla chips instead of toilet paper or sandpaper instead of a bath towel?

394

...have your hair cut by someone who's blindfolded or have to cut someone else's hair while you're blindfolded?

395

...be trapped for three days in a library or a gym?

396

...see everything in orange or have every food taste the same?

397

...swim in a pool of sour milk or sit in a bath with rotting fish?

398

...be a flower or a tree?

399

...eat a banana peel or an orange peel?

400

...eat for free for the rest of your life but have it be food you don't like, or only eat food you love but have to pay five times the normal price for it?

401

...hug a koala bear or a panda?

402

...be an octopus or a crab?

403

...take a train in India or a bus in South America?

404

...use toothpaste that smells like garlic or body wash that smells like fish?

405

...have to paint the Brooklyn Bridge or clean the Statue of Liberty?

406

...only eat food that's so spicy it burns your mouth or food that's so bland it has no flavor?

407

...have to wear a T-shirt when it's cold or a sweatshirt when it's hot?

408

...have to use your hands to eat ice cream or soup?

409

...own a lightsaber or a Batmobile?

410

...build a scale model of the Eiffel Tower out of matchsticks or the Golden Gate Bridge out of uncooked spaghetti?

411

...be a baby or an old person?

412

...have a beach outside your house that's always filled with noisy tourists or live ten miles from a beach that no one goes to?

413

...hold a tarantula on your hand or have a snake around your neck?

414

...be a lamppost that a dog pees on or a windscreen that a bird poops on?

415

...cut down a tree using a steak knife or empty a swimming pool using a coffee cup?

416

...see a ghost or a mummy?

417

...have a job taste-testing pizza or testing video games?

418

...wake up and find you're in a foreign country where you don't speak the language or be lost in a rainforest?

419

...have everyone always stare at you or have no one ever look at you?

420

...go on a bike ride or go swimming?

421

...have rain be made of paint or snow be made of mud?

422

...have it rain or snow every day?

423

...own a cat or a dog?

424

...be good at sport or math?

425

...travel by camel or elephant?

426

...eat at a seafood restaurant overlooking the ocean or at a rooftop restaurant overlooking a city?

427

...visit Hogwarts or Willy Wonka's chocolate factory?

428

...lie to your best friend or have them lie to you?

429

...drink from a can or a bottle?

430

...live without your phone or without internet access?

431

...appear in only one movie and win an Oscar or appear in 100 movies and never win an Oscar?

432

...have no shadow or no reflection?

433

...walk for 20 miles or ride a bicycle for 100 miles?

434

...eat straight fries or curly fries?

435

...carve a pumpkin or go on a hayride?

436

...have a carrot for a nose or sticks for your arms?

437

...step on a plug or a piece of Lego?

438

...go swimming with penguins or seals?

439

...not be able to smell anything or not be able to taste anything?

440

...have to remain standing or lying down for the rest of your life?

441

...lick the inside of someone's ear or their armpit?

442

...go skiing or snowboarding?

443

...chew someone else's hair or suck their thumb?

444

...jump into a trash can outside a fast food restaurant or step in dog poop while barefoot?

445

...run a marathon with shoes or a 5k race barefoot?

446

...have it be 50°F or 120°F all summer?

447

...have a bad haircut or ugly clothes?

448

...wear a crash helmet in bed or sleep sitting upright?

449

...have one of your teeth fall out every year or go bald overnight?

450

...meet Gandalf or Dumbledore?

451

...complete a project as part of a team or by yourself?

452

...put your head in a lion's mouth or waterski over a shark tank?

453

...sweep the floor or mop the floor?

454

...live somewhere with lots of tornadoes or lots of earthquakes?

455

...be trapped in the earwax or boogers of a giant?

456

...be able to speak one other language fluently or have a basic grasp of five other languages?

457

...run a farm that keeps llamas or ostriches?

458

...wash dishes or dry dishes?

459

...bite your tongue or stub your toe?

460

...mow the yard when it's 110°F outside or shovel the snow from the driveway when it's 10°F?

461

...marry someone you don't love but who loves you or marry someone you do love but who doesn't love you?

462

...build a snowman or make a snow angel?

463

...write a bestselling novel or sing a bestselling song?

464

...learn a new word every day or create a new language?

465

...go shopping for food the day before Thanksgiving or for gifts the day before Christmas?

466

...fall off the catwalk at a fashion show or forget the words of the national anthem when singing at the President's inauguration?

467

...talk in your sleep or sleepwalk?

468

...need to sneeze and not be able to or need to cough and not be able to?

469

...appear on a billboard in Times Square for one day or on a billboard in your local city for a year?

470

...hike up a mountain or along a river?

471

...wake up three times a night to pee or have to pee 25 times during the day?

472

...live once for 500 years or five times for 100 years each?

473

...hear someone behind you while walking alone in the dark or hear a tapping on the window when you're watching a scary movie at home by yourself?

474

...have $100 or have your face on every $100 bill?

475

...know the date you'll die or have no idea?

476

...come from a rich family and have parents who don't love you or come from a poor family and have parents who do love you?

477

...be the last human alive or be dead?

478

...go sailing or kayaking?

479

...have to make a shelter using tree branches or have to start a fire by rubbing two sticks together?

480

...be an only child or have five siblings?

481

...volunteer at an animal shelter or a homeless shelter?

482

...sing in a karaoke contest or take part in a spelling bee?

483

...work in an office or work outside?

484

...be stuck in traffic for five hours or pay $50 to avoid it by using a toll road?

485

...be able to create fire at will or have X-ray vision?

486

...ride an ostrich or a camel?

487

...be in a classroom with 30 people or by yourself getting one-to-one tutoring?

488

...give the wrong answer in class or call your teacher "Mom"?

489

...be known for being encouraging or for being generous?

490

...go to school every day for rest of your life or never have had an opportunity to learn anything?

491

...be the first person to discover unicorns or aliens?

492

...stand on the edge of a tall building or fly in a helicopter which has its doors open?

493

...read the Harry Potter books or watch the movies?

494

...eat corn flakes covered with cold baked beans or carrots covered in ketchup?

495

...have three months off school for summer or one month off three times throughout the year?

496

...eat pizza with a thin crust or thick crust?

497

...go skydiving or bungee jumping?

498

...see a shark or a 100 foot wave while surfing?

499

...be able to climb a tree like a squirrel or dig burrows like a mole?

500

...sit on a rocking chair or a leather couch?

501

...wear glasses or contact lenses?

OTHER HELPFUL RESOURCES

Youth Workin' It

If you work with children or teens, Youth Workin' It has all the ideas you could ever need – games, session plans, other activities, fundraisers and much more.

youthworkinit.com

Riddles For Kids

Riddles For Kids has hundreds of riddles based on many different themes – perfect for all kinds of different activities.

riddles-for-kids.org

Scavenger Hunt

Scavenger Hunt has hundreds of scavenger hunt ideas and includes free printable worksheets for you to use.

scavenger-hunt.org

Made in the USA
Middletown, DE
24 October 2018